Dear Family,

What's the b...... your chi........

..... e this ..... d read

Here are ...e tips.

●**Take a "picture walk."** Look at all the pictures before you read. Talk about what you see.

●**Take turns.** Read to your child. Ham it up! Use different voices for different characters, and read with feeling! Then listen as your child reads to you, or explains the story in his or her own words.

●**Point out words as you read.** Help your child notice how letters and sounds go together. Point out unusual or difficult words that your child might not know. Talk about those words and what they mean.

●**Ask questions.** Stop to ask questions as you read. For example: "What do you think will happen next?" "How would you feel if that happened to you?"

●**Read every day.** Good stories are worth reading more than once! Read signs, labels, and even cereal boxes with your child. Visit the library to take out more books. And look for other JUST FOR YOU! BOOKS you and your child can share!

The Editors

For my sister, Vivian.
—RB

This book is for my family—who gave me
roots to cling to and wings to fly.
—MB

Text copyright © 2004 by Regina Brooks.
Illustrations copyright © 2004 by Marjorie Borgella.
Produced for Scholastic by COLOR-BRIDGE BOOKS, LLC, Brooklyn, NY
All rights reserved. Published by SCHOLASTIC INC.
JUST FOR YOU! is a trademark of Scholastic Inc.

No part of this publication may be reproduced in whole or in part, or stored in a
retrieval system, or transmitted in any form or by any means, electronic, mechanical,
photocopying, recording, or otherwise, without written permission of the publisher.
For information regarding permission, write to Scholastic Inc.,
557 Broadway, New York, NY 10012.

Library of Congress Cataloging-in-Publication Data

Brooks, Regina.
    Never finished, never done!/by Regina Brooks; illustrated by Marjorie Borgella.
        p. cm.—(Just for you! Level 2)
    Summary: Momma asks Shayla to set the table, pick up her toys, and feed
the cat before the family can go to play in the park on a Saturday morning.
    ISBN 0-439-56863-3
    [1. Work—Fiction. 2. Play—Fiction. 3. Family life—Fiction. 4. Stories in
    rhyme.] I. Borgella, Marjorie, ill. II. Title. III. Series.
    PZ8.3.B7897Ne 2004
    [Fic]—dc22   2004004768

15 14 13 12 11 10 9 8   11 12 13 14
        Printed in the U.S.A. 40 • First Scholastic Printing, April 2004

Never Finished, Never Done!

by Regina Brooks

Illustrated by Marjorie Borgella

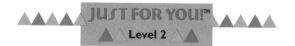

Momma, Momma!
It's Saturday!
How long before we go?

We'll leave for the park
in no time, Shayla—
if you don't move
too slow!

It's Saturday morning.
We're supposed to have fun.
But we have so many chores to do,
I don't think we'll ever get done.

Find your red shirt and sneakers.
Make sure you have clean socks.
Then pick up all your toys, please,
and put them in the toy box.

Don't just come in the kitchen
and grab yourself a seat!
The table must be nicely set
before you sit down to eat.

The fork goes on the left side—
knife and spoon go on the other.
Wash the dishes after breakfast,
while I bathe your baby brother.

Girl, you must have been hungry!
You really cleaned your plate.
We'll get to the park in no time
if we keep going at this rate!

Help me sort the dirty clothes—
two piles—light and dark.
I'll put them in the washing machine
before we leave for the park.

Chores, chores, chores!
Will they ever get done?
There are so many chores to do,
I'll never have any fun.

Don't show me that lip,
and you'd better make haste!
Please hurry up, Shayla—
and fix your face.

Pick out the beads
you'd like to wear.
Then come and sit down,
and I'll braid your hair.

Now make up your bed,
and be sure the sheets are clean.

My goodness, Momma!
You've got me working
like a machine!

I'll never finish.
I'll never get done.
I'll never get a chance
to play in the sun.

I want to go to the park
with the rest of my crew.
This is way too much work
for one person to do.

This list is taking much too long—
Momma, it's just not fair!

You're doing such a great job!
Shayla, we're almost there.

If you do these chores now—
you won't have to do them later.
Your momma's not raising
a pro-cras-tin-a-tor.

Shayla, won't you please
stop complaining?

Momma, I'm just explaining!
Just when I think my chores are done,
here you come with another one.

23

Please feed the cat
while I clean his litter.
Then grab your brother's bag,
and we'll take him to the sitter.

Chores, chores, chores!
Will they ever get done?
My little brother can't help—
he's barely one.
Never finished!
Never done!

I'm finished!
We're ready!
I'm heading out the door.

Aaaaaw, snap!
Here comes Momma
with another chore!

★ Get Dressed
★ Pick Up Toys
★ Set Table
★ Wash Dishes
★ Sort Laundry
★ Braid Hair
★ Make Up Bed
★ Feed Cat

You have stars on your list, Shayla.
We're finally done.
You really are finished.
Let's go have some fun!

YES!

▲▲▲▲▲▲ JUST FOR YOU ▲▲▲▲▲▲

Here are some fun things for you to do.

Never Say Never!

Shayla says, "Never finished. Never done!"
Why does she say that?

Think of a time when YOU had to do a chore that you didn't want to do.

Did you feel as if you would never finish?

How did you feel when you did finish?

Write a funny story about doing that chore.
You can call YOUR story "Never Say Never!"

★ Get Dressed
★ Pick Up Toys
★ Set Table
★ Wash Dishes
★ Sort Laundry
★ Braid Hair
★ Make Up Bed
★ Feed Cat

Stars for YOU!

What chores do YOU do to help out at home?

Do you clean your room?
Set the table?
Feed a pet?
Help take care of a little brother or sister?

Make a list of all the ways YOU help out.

Give yourself a star for each chore you do!

YOUR Day at the Park

Why do you think Shayla is in such a hurry to get to the park?

Pretend that YOU are Shayla's friend, and you are waiting for her at the park. Will you two play on the swings, or go skating, or play ball?

Draw a picture to show what you will do together. What happens in the park is up to YOU!

▲▲▲▲TOGETHER TIME ▲▲▲▲

Make some time to share ideas about the story with your young reader! Here are some activities you can try. There are no right or wrong answers!

Talk About It: Shayla's mother says, "If you do these chores now—you won't have to do them later. Your momma's not raising a pro-cras-tin-a-tor." Explain to your child that a procrastinator is someone who puts off doing something that needs to get done. Is anyone in your family a procrastinator? (There's usually at least one in every family!) Talk about how other family members can help this person get things done faster!

Think About It: Ask your child, "Why do you think Shayla's mother asked her to do so many things? Would Shayla and her mother have been able to get to the park any earlier if Shayla had not helped out and done so many chores? Why?"

Read It Again: Rhymes and the realistic conversation between Shayla and her mother make this story fun to read. You can have even more fun by reading the story aloud as if it were a play. Give your child the chance to read Momma's part and act out being in charge! You can ham it up as you read Shayla's dialogue.

Meet the Author

REGINA BROOKS says, "As a child I could never understand those chores you had to do over and over again—like washing the dishes or making your bed. My favorite chores were raking leaves and shoveling snow. I could do them outside with my sister! In Rochester, we had many trees and always got lots of snow during the winter. Although I liked raking and shoveling, just when I thought I was done, the wind would blow down more leaves or a blizzard would bring more snow. But that was okay because it meant more piles of leaves to jump in, more hills to sled down, and more snowmen to build."

Regina Brooks grew up in Rochester, New York, and attended the School of the Arts there. She graduated from Ohio State University with a bachelor's degree in Aerospace Engineering. She now lives in Brooklyn, New York, where she works as a literary agent and writer. *Never Finished, Never Done!* is her first children's book.

▲▲▲▲▲▲▲▲▲▲▲▲▲▲▲▲▲▲▲▲

Meet the Artist

MARJORIE BORGELLA says, "I'm the youngest of four girls in my family. When my older sisters went to school, I had nobody to play with. So I had to learn to play all by myself—and have fun! On cold winter days when I couldn't go outside, I entertained myself. I began drawing and painting in kindergarten, and it became my favorite thing to do all the time!"

Marjorie Borgella was born to Haitian parents in Brooklyn, New York. She went to the High School of Art & Design, and received a Bachelor of Fine Arts Degree in Illustration from the Parsons School of Design in 1997. She now lives in the Caribbean on the sunny island of Antigua. She loves coming home to Brooklyn to visit her family, but she enjoys living in a place where she is able to paint outdoors every day if she wants to.